DISNEYLAND PARIS TRAVEL GUIDE FOR FIRST-TIMERS

Everything You Need to Know to Make the Most of Your Disneyland Paris Vacation.

Jerry J. Howard

Copyright © Jerry J. Howard, 2023.

All rights reserved. Before this document is duplicated or reproduced in any manner, the publisher's consent must be gained. Therefore, the contents within can neither be stored electronically, transferred, nor kept in a database. Neither in Part nor full can the document be copied, scanned, faxed, or retained without approval from the publisher or creator.

Table of Contents

Introduction 6

Chapter 1: Overview of Disneyland Paris 7

    Hotel Zone 7

    How to Travel from Paris to Disneyland Paris 7

    The Best Airports for Disneyland Paris 8

Chapter 2: When to Visit Disneyland Paris? 9

Chapter 3: Planning Your Trip 12

    Accommodations Close to Disneyland Paris 12

        On-Property Disney World Paris Hotels 12

        Off-Property Accommodations Near Disneyland Paris 14

    Dining at Disneyland Paris 14

    Important Dining Lessons and Advice 16

Chapter 4: Disneyland Paris Budget Tips 17

    A Description of the Resort 17

    The Best Value Disney Hotels 18

    Discount Tickets 19

    The Most Affordable (Good) Food 20

Chapter 5: Avoiding Long Lines at Disneyland Paris 22

Why Is It a Good Idea to Avoid the Lines at Disneyland Paris? 22

Visitor Advice 24

Chapter 6: The Parks 26

Disneyland Park 26

Walt Disney Studios Park 27

Chapter 7: What to Bring to Disneyland Paris 28

What to Bring and Wear at Disneyland Paris 28

Common Questions Regarding Visiting Disneyland Paris 29

Are Both Parks Accessible in a Single Day? 29

Is The Single Rider Option Available? 29

Is FastPass Available? 29

What Is the Current State of Disneyland Paris? 30

Parade at Disneyland Paris 30

Where else is near Disneyland Paris? 30

Tips for Disneyland Paris 31

Chapter 8: Lost at Disney! 35

What to Do at Disney if Your Child Gets Lost 35

Chapter 9: How to Take Great Photos at Disneyland Paris 38

3

Making A Memorable Disney Video with Your Family. 43

Tips for Disney Videos 45

Chapter 10: Disneyland for Young Children 46

Questions and Answers 55

Can a 2-year-old have fun in Disney World?..........55

Where in Disney World Should Toddlers Spend Their Time? 56

How Can a Disney Vacation Be Arranged with A Toddler? 56

Are Toddlers Allowed to Visit Disney World?.......57

Chapter 11: Disneyland for Adults 58

The Top Disneyland Tips for Adults.........................59

Why would an adult go to Disneyland? 59

When Adults Should Visit Disneyland 59

Which amusement park, California Adventure or Disneyland, is more suitable for adults? 60

What Should an Adult Bring to Disneyland? 61

The Best Adult Activities at Disneyland....................62

The Best Rides at Disneyland for Adults 62

Adults' Top Thrill Rides at Disneyland 63

Adults' Coolest Disneyland Rides 65

4

Chapter 12: Best Disneyland Paris Rides 67

Chapter 13: How Many Days Should You Plan to Visit Disneyland Paris? 69

Bonus Chapter: Disneyland Paris Itinerary 70

Travel Journal: For Jotting Down Unforgettable Encounters 76

Introduction

Our family has vacationed at Disney World and Disneyland quite a bit, like many other families. However, we enjoy branching out and seeing places other than Disney resorts.

On our first trip to Europe with the kids, we spent two weeks in the UK and France this summer. While the majority of our trip was spent visiting historical and cultural places, we all knew we needed some fun to balance out the churches and museums. Of course, we had to include a stop at Disneyland Paris in our itinerary.

As a frequent visitor to the American Disney parks, I had a hunch that our expertise would be put to good use at Disneyland Paris as well. I was aware that we still had a lot to learn. In its international parks, Disney has put in place extremely varied policies and procedures. When we took our oldest to Disneyland Paris and Hong Kong Disneyland years ago, we learned that we needed to do our research.

The only overseas Disney property that many tourists have been able to visit easily in recent months is Disneyland Paris, as travel to China is still basically impossible for the foreseeable future and Japan is only just beginning to open up. As a result, (and especially due to the resort's ongoing 30th anniversary in 2022–2023), Americans and Canadians have recently shown a lot of interest in Disneyland Paris. As Paris prepares to host the 2024 Summer Olympics, there will probably be even more.

Here is everything you need to know and plan for if you are a tourist familiar with American theme parks thinking about visiting Disneyland Paris, from accommodations to line-cutting techniques to transportation advice.

Chapter 1: Overview of Disneyland Paris

Hotel Zone

There is a hotel section of the park with six hotels if you are visiting Disneyland from a greater distance and are in France as opposed to Paris. Although they are a little further from the rest of Disneyland Park, there are two other newer hotels.

How to Travel from Paris to Disneyland Paris

The best way to get to the parks for visitors coming from or going to central Paris is via rail. The Marne-la-Vallée-Chessy station, which is close to the parks, is where the RER (Regional Express Network) line A exits. On maps, look for the red line. You must ensure that you are boarding the correct train on the correct platform because line A separates. Fortunately, the station signs are well labelled with adorable Mickey heads, making navigation simple.

We had the good fortune to be staying in Paris close to the line A station, Châtelet Les Halles. The trip to Disneyland Paris was extremely simple from this starting point. The trip takes about 40 minutes and costs only €5 for adults (kids under 4 ride free, and those between the ages of 4 and 10 pay half the price). Keep your ticket handy—you'll need it to leave the station once you get there.

You can also take a cab or an Uber from the city center, but they will cost you much more and might take longer due to traffic.

The Best Airports for Disneyland Paris

The Charles de Gaulle Airport (CDG) in Paris is the nearest to Disneyland Paris for passengers arriving or departing by air. We immediately left the parks to take a flight to Scotland, where we were going next in Europe. Since we had numerous heavier bags to carry, we simply got an Uber from our hotel to CDG. Our entire cost for the about 35–40-minute trip, which included ordering a larger van, was €77.

TGV Train: The high-speed train takes just ten minutes to get to CDG, but it is infrequent, complicated, and expensive.

Magical Shuttle: As part of your vacation package, Disneyland Paris will transport you by motor coach for an extra cost. Transfers can take up to 60 minutes, but for visitors who don't want to navigate everything on their own, this is a simple option.

Paris-Orly (ORY): Another significant airport, is another option for visitors flying to Disneyland Paris. The parks are roughly a 45-minute drive from ORY. Although a train from Orly to Disneyland Paris necessitates passing through the heart of Paris, the Magical Shuttle is also accessible there.

Chapter 2: When to Visit Disneyland Paris?

We strongly advise visiting Disneyland Paris in the spring, fall, or winter if you have a choice of dates and seasons, especially during the shoulder seasons outside of France's busiest travel times. In particular, we adore Christmas at Disneyland Paris. As long as you avoid Christmas week through New Year's Eve, this is a terrific time to come.

Because of the crowds and previous heat waves that have swept through Europe the past few summers, we normally advise avoiding the months of June through August. The Lion King Jungle Festival, which receives high praise, is the sole drawback of not traveling during the summer. The bad weather and throngs of people, however, are worthless.

Speaking of which, we discover that April and May, as well as late September through November, are the finest months for the weather in Paris. These are the most comfortable times of the year, and while it can snow in the winter, mid-November often isn't very cold. Mid- to Late-December, however, might be pushing your luck.

Christmas is a great time to visit Disneyland Paris and Walt Disney Studios Park because of the abundance of extra seasonal activities and the lovely decorations that are displayed around the park. Additionally, the atmosphere of the City of Paris during the festive season is unrivaled.

There's also the decision of whether to go now or wait till later if you're thinking more long-term. As part of a $2.5 billion makeover of the Walt Disney Studios Park, Disneyland Paris has ambitious long-term intentions.

Prior to the 2024 Summer Olympics in Paris, the Walt Disney Studios Park will undergo a series of phases of reconstruction. Avengers Campus, which launched last summer, was the first part to open. After that, the Kingdom of Arendelle will presumably debut around 2024. (Star Wars: Galaxy's Edge may or may not still be developed as part of the Walt Disney Studios Park extension; however, this is not certain.)

The majority of the expansion will be completed prior to the Summer Olympics in Paris in 2024, making the spring of 2024 the likely "best" period to visit. You'll beat the Olympic crowds, and all of this expansion will be completed. However, the majority of people who are reading this right now aren't making travel arrangements for a few years from now. More so, you are debating whether or not you ought to travel to France this year. In such a situation, it doesn't really matter that much.

Of course, France is much more than Disneyland Paris, so you should also schedule your trip to coincide with the optimal time to see the other places on your itinerary. Our second favorite city in the world is Paris, and we strongly suggest visiting for at least a few days.

I strongly advise visiting other parts of France as well as other countries in Europe! In my France Travel Guide for First Timers on Amazon.com, I provided in-depth travel advice. Planning for the remaining days of your holiday can start there.

We've been all over Europe, including the French areas of Normandy, the Loire Valley, and the Côte d'Azur. We've visited Norway, Denmark, Switzerland, Austria, Italy, Germany, and the United Kingdom in addition to France.

Even though we adore Disney and Disneyland Paris, many of these other actual places have been the most memorable parts of our travels. Amazing locations abound in Europe, leaving a lasting impression on travelers. At Disneyland Paris, there is truly something for everyone outside of the parks. There is definitely something for everyone, from history to contemporary culture to seedy red-light districts (since we're so sure Disney lovers are like that sort of thing!).

Let's get preparing if this has you considering a trip to Europe to see Disneyland Paris and other memorable cultural attractions, or if you were already considering going and want more details and advice.

Chapter 3: Planning Your Trip

Accommodations Close to Disneyland Paris

On-Property Disney World Paris Hotels

The Disneyland Paris Resort consists of seven Disney-owned hotel establishments. They consist of (roughly speaking, from most expensive to least expensive):

- The Disneyland Paris Hotel
- Hotel New York – Art of Marvel
- Newport Bay Club
- Sequoia Lodge
- Hotel Santa Fe
- Hotel Cheyenne
- Davy Crockett Ranch (campground)

No matter where you decide to stay, most families will undoubtedly need to modify their expectations for Disney hotels in terms of price as well as service and amenities. The hotel issue, in our opinion, was the poorest aspect of our trip to Disneyland Paris because we are used to what Disneyland and Disney World have to offer.

The main hotel in the same vein as the Grand Floridian or Hong Kong Disneyland Hotel is the Disneyland Paris Hotel. It has by far the best location of the group because it is located directly above the gates to Disneyland Park. Unfortunately, it wasn't open in 2022 due to renovations. It just received word that it might reopen sometime around 2024. The other hotels are currently feeling the effects of this closure. If it had been open, this is probably where we would have stayed, regardless of the cost. Beautiful home with a significant location advantage over the competition.

The Hotel New York redesign by Art of Marvel was just completed in 2021. I've heard from reliable sources that it is quite stylish and well-themed. However, it can still cost up to $800–900 per night for a modestly sized accommodation with two double (not queen!) beds. That was unacceptable to our family. Furthermore, this hotel is farther away from the theme parks than the Disneyland Hotel is, requiring a 15- to 20-minute walk through Disney Village to get there.

Our family gave the Newport Bay Club and Sequoia Lodge, both of which are located just a few minutes' walk from Hotel New York, careful consideration for our trip. We frequently stayed at the Orlando Yacht and Beach Club before it underwent renovations, but the Newport Bay Club is pretty comparable, so we chose to save a little more money and stay at Sequoia Lodge. (We determined that the longer walk to the parks did not make the additional discounts offered by Hotel Santa Fe or Hotel Cheyenne worthwhile.)

Sequoia Lodge, like Wilderness Lodge in Orlando or the Grand Californian in Anaheim, is designed to resemble a classic national park lodge. However, it is not at all a luxurious property like those hotels. It is a moderately priced hotel at Disneyland Paris.

The accommodations, on the other hand, didn't seem to us to be quite as nice as many of the freshly refurbished discount resorts at Walt Disney World. Again, ordinary rooms only have two double beds, so we determined that in order for our family of four to sleep properly, we would need to reserve two rooms. Although the hotel's public spaces may have been a little nicer, Sequoia Lodge was a rather poor value overall.

Off-Property Accommodations Near Disneyland Paris

There are several off-property hotel options if these Disney hotels don't sound like your cup of tea due to their restrictions. Many are found in the Marne-la-Vallée area.

Some of these are close to the retail mall Val d'Europe, while others are not far away. Some of these hotels and Disney have partnered to offer packages that can be purchased through the Disneyland Paris website.

The Radisson Blu Hotel Paris, Marne-la-Vallée, or Marriott's Village d'ile-de-France are also fantastic choices if you're looking for more opulent lodging at a lower cost.

However, keep in mind that if you stay off-site, you'll miss out on the main benefit of on-property lodging, which is early However, you'll probably save some cash and benefit from superior lodging and/or more space.

Dining at Disneyland Paris

Plaza Gardens Restaurant Buffet Disneyland Paris

The Plaza Gardens buffet caught me off guard, but the majority of the cuisine at Disneyland Paris is mediocre.

The food options in Disney parks are usually pretty fantastic, and France as a whole is a gourmet paradise. So many guests to Disneyland Paris anticipate that combining those two will result in some incredible gastronomy. Unfortunately, Disneyland Paris totally falls short on the cuisine aspect. You should be ready for visitors so that food is not the main focus of your time, effort, or resources!

At least among Disney enthusiasts, it is well known that the food at Disneyland Paris is subpar. Our family was therefore forewarned, and we made appropriate preparations for supper.

However, we were pleasantly surprised to see that the meals at the counter were more than adequate. The meal wasn't significantly better or worse than that at counter-service restaurants at Walt Disney World or Disneyland. At Au Chalet de la Marionnette, we enjoyed some tasty sausages and fries; at Stark Factory on Avengers Campus, we enjoyed some tasty pizza and spaghetti; and at Plaza Gardens, we were pleasantly surprised by the lunch buffet.

The meals served at tables were where the reputation for poor food was most prevalent. My husband and I went to Captain Jack's, which had a restaurant with a view of Pirates of the Caribbean that resembled Blue Bayou at Disneyland, just to see for ourselves. They both agreed that the dish was overdone and flavorless and that it was excessively pricey. We were relieved that we didn't pay for a table for all four of us.

Additionally, American visitors to Disneyland Paris should be prepared for a somewhat small selection of snack alternatives. Evidently, they haven't caught on to the trend of creating new Instagrammable delicacies every other week. Instead, you'll probably discover a few quite unimpressive ice cream bars and simple nibbles like chips and popcorn.

Important Dining Lessons and Advice

Here are some additional crucial pointers for guests to understand regarding food and dining:

Make your arrangements 60 days in advance. Reservations for table service meals at Disneyland Paris are available 60 days in advance, including character dining. These do fill up quickly, so be sure to set a calendar reminder for yourself (and be aware of time zone changes).

Try walkups: If you don't have a reservation at a buffet or table service restaurant, try showing up a few minutes early to see if you can get a seat as a walkup. Both times we tried it, it worked for us.

At Disneyland Paris, a surprising number of counter-service restaurants close even before the dinner hour. To ensure that you don't miss the opportunity to eat where you'd choose, carefully check the hours.

Consider dining outside of the parks because Disney Village offers more selections than the parks, particularly for dinner. As a result, if all else fails, eat there (preferably before or after dinner, as lines might be long).

Chapter 4: Disneyland Paris Budget Tips

It's difficult to put into words the wonder that surrounds Disneyland Paris. It's a daring and distinctive approach to Disney that manages to keep some of Disneyland's most enduring features.

Visiting this European fantasy is a must for any Disney lover, and it's on many people's bucket lists. However, if money is tight, don't let that stop you from having the trip of a lifetime.

Here are some fantastic ways to save money at Disneyland Paris and make your trip more enjoyable.

A Description of the Resort

Spend some time learning more about the resort and the associated charges before you begin planning your Disneyland Paris budget.

In general, Disney vacation packages handle practically everything for you. The majority of the time, your resort will be close to the parks, and a shuttle to the parks will be provided as part of your accommodation rate.

There are two parks; the main one is Disneyland Park, but Walt Disney Studios is also expanding quickly. For Pixar and Marvel attractions, it has emerged as the go-to location. Arendelle from the Frozen film series will appear in a new expansion that will debut the following year.

Make sure you allow enough time for these parks as well as any additional entertainment, excursions, and activities you choose to include in your trip to Disneyland Paris. My main piece of advice is to start with a budget before moving on to all the cost-effective Disneyland Paris budget ideas.

If you don't know where the top is, taking money from the top is useless. Right?

The Best Value Disney Hotels

The cost of lodging is the largest component of a Disney vacation. You can reduce the cost of your trip by hundreds, if not thousands, if you save money on the accommodations. There are several different accommodation alternatives at Disneyland Paris, some of which are substantially more affordable.

Saving money on your hotel is one of my favorite Disneyland Paris spending suggestions. Paying for extras you won't use or need is wasteful. That significantly lowers the cost. The most important thing is to choose a cheap hotel, as long as your stay won't suffer as a result.

You could want to extend your trip, as I indicated before, and paying less for lodging makes that possible. If you choose more luxury, think about cutting your stay short with a shorter itinerary.

There are two methods for finding a cheap hotel at Disneyland Paris. Both the Hotel Cheyenne (to conjure up Woody's Round Up) and the Hotel Santa Fe (to conjure up Cars) are reasonably priced.

They are affordable choices. compared to the pricier Disney lodgings.

However, by booking a hotel just ten minutes away from Disney, you can save a lot more money. To receive the best deals, you must book non-Disney hotels directly rather than via Disney.

Although Davy Crockett Ranch is less expensive, you will need a car to get there because there are no transportation options to the park. As a result, you will need to drive to the park each time you go.

We've been at the Ranch twice, and the trip between Davy Crockett and the Parks is straightforward, although it depends on each person's level of driving comfort.

Although it is simpler to make your reservations through Disney, you can save money by doing some research on the resorts nearby. Pay attention to the amenities and services that are vital to you.

A large playground may not be very useful if you don't stay at the hotel very long. Some hotels provide incredibly useful amenities like free breakfast and park shuttle service.

Discount Tickets

Purchasing discounted tickets from a reputable third-party reseller is another option to save, similar to making your hotel reservation separately. Picnic offers reduced tickets for Disneyland Paris, which will ultimately increase your revenue.

Before you reserve your vacation package, you can also find special discounts on the Disneyland Paris website. 365 Tickets is known for carrying a wide selection of seats at cheap prices.

Saving money on entrance isn't limited to purchasing discounted tickets. I also have further financial advice for Disneyland Paris connected to tickets.

When comparing ticket prices, take your time. The dates you choose will affect the price, and a single day can result in considerable savings. When choosing the kind of tickets to buy, you should give it some serious thought as well.

Disney+
Disney Bundle
Sponsored by Disney+
For one unbelievable price, you can access epic stories, a ton of films and TV episodes, and more.

With each additional day, the average cost of multi-day passes decreases. These tickets, however, are expensive park-hopping tickets.

The cost is much more than a single-day one-park ticket, even after lowering the average price per day. Ironically, a shorter journey maximizes the value of these two-park passes while increasing the cost per ticket.

The majority of the time, choosing one park and spending the day there makes the most sense. Walt Disney Studios and Disneyland, in my opinion, are each worth one day.

Choosing not to pay for Premier access to well-known attractions is another method to save money. If the price is within your budget or if moving forward with with your schedule will save you a night's hotel, you can justify the expense.

Unless there is a brand-new ride with an unacceptable wait time, it is typically an extra cost that provides little to enhance your experience. Definitely, only on busy days do I advise it.

The Most Affordable (Good) Food

The easiest way to save money on food is to eat as often as possible at quick-service restaurants. There are fewer "rules," so you can not only save on less expensive meals, but you can also buy shareable meals to save even more. If you have a little appetite, you can even order from the kid's menu.

If you have multiple young children, splitting the dinners and adding some homemade snacks is a terrific way to stretch your budget.

When making your travel arrangements, be sure to research the most recent specials available. Half-board accommodations, which include breakfast and dinner as well as lunch, may prove to be more cost-effective.

A lot of the packages also come with a drink, either hot or cold, and a snack pass that may be used to buy an ice cream cone or a sweet pastry. Our kids adored their snack and occasionally inquired about it more than they did about their actual meals!

Bringing your own snacks to the park is another way to save money on food. Absolutely fine, and I advise it as a means to increase your financial savings. If you become hungry and there isn't a restaurant open nearby, it can also save your life.

But I do advise bringing at least some of your own non-alcoholic drinks. Bring the small pouches of concentrated squash to add to the water at the park's numerous drinking fountains, and of course, a proper water bottle to contain the beverage.

Consider carrying sweaters or coats into the park with you so you won't feel the need to buy additional gear to stay warm.

The same rule applies to hats and sunglasses, unless you have enough money to purchase them as keepsakes.

Chapter 5: Avoiding Long Lines at Disneyland Paris

If you're in France, don't miss the magnificent experience that is Disneyland Paris. It is the largest theme park in Europe and genuinely has some of the top rides and attractions with a Disney theme for visitors of all ages to enjoy. About 12 million tourists visit it annually due to its proximity to the global center of fashion and its distinctive French flair, making it the ideal place to go with friends and family. Continue reading to learn how to avoid lengthy waiting lines at Disneyland Paris for a stress-free and enjoyable trip.

Why Is It a Good Idea to Avoid the Lines at Disneyland Paris?

Whenever possible, stay away from large crowds. As the largest theme park in Europe, Disneyland Paris is a very popular tourist destination and draws huge crowds to enjoy its charm. Therefore, learn how to cut lines to enjoy a hassle-free experience.

Avoid long lines at Disneyland Paris, where several of the park's iconic and unique attractions have wait times of up to an hour.

Enjoy the expansive parks. There is never enough time to experience Disneyland Paris's two theme parks to their fullest. You will undoubtedly want some advice on how to skip the lines, with over 50 rides and attractions offering you an enthralling and exhilarating expericncc.

Spiking lineups at attractions can allow you more time to meet and greet your favorite Disney characters. Spend more time with your favorite characters.

(1) Purchase Tickets Online
The largest and most well-known theme park in all of Europe, Disneyland Paris features a number of distinctive rides and attractions with a French flair. Disney enthusiasts come from all over the world to enjoy Disneyland Paris' French magic. Although purchasing tickets at the counter can be a nightmare, there is a solution. Purchase Disneyland Paris tickets online to avoid huge lineups at the entrances and enter the theme parks without fuss.

2. Reserve A Room in A Disneyland Paris Hotel
The hotels at Disneyland Paris provide a number of alluring advantages. You can benefit from exclusive entrance to the theme parks in addition to getting free parking and a wonderful stay in hotels decorated in classic Disney themes. Extra Magic Time is a service that allows guests staying at a Disney hotel to enjoy the rides and attractions before the regular opening times without standing in line. Additionally, you are free to visit Disneyland Paris whenever you like, day or night. By staying at hotels near Disneyland Paris, you can also get discounts on park admission.

3. Pay A Visit in The Early Morning
By coming to Disneyland Paris as soon as the parks open in the morning, you can avoid line-ups. You may enjoy the rides and attractions at Disneyland Paris in peace and quiet, with fewer visitors and shorter queues. You can avoid squeezing through large crowds and spend some fun one-on-one time with your favorite Disney characters, such as Mickey Mouse and the princesses at Princess Pavillion, by getting there early.

4. Stay Past the Parks Closing Time.
Just before closing time is the optimum time to enjoy the rides and attractions at Disneyland Paris. Two hours before the park closes, a large percentage of the throng disperses, providing you the ideal window of time to skip waiting lines and take full advantage of your favorite attractions. Your experience will be unique and

unforgettable thanks to the starry night sky and Disneyland's bright lighting.

5. Choose Disney Premier Access.
You have priority access to particular attractions at Disneyland Paris with Disney Premier Access. This may be purchased online through the Disneyland Paris app or at the park's ticket booth and functions exactly like a top-up to your normal park ticket. You can speed through attractions one by one or have a supercharged day. Even a single purchase of Premier Access for one attraction within a specific time period is possible. You can only use Disney Premier Access if you have admission to both Disney parks. Only certain attractions are faster to access thanks to this facility. It does not ensure quick access.

6. Sign Up as A Disney Single Rider.
By using the SINGLE RIDER service, you may pack as much magic into your visit to Disneyland Paris as you like. Free service Single Rider can significantly shorten wait times. All you need to do is be prepared to ride and see sites alone. You won't have a choice of seat or vehicle, despite the fact that rides and attractions have a distinct entrance. This service is for you if you're okay with spending time at rides and attractions by yourself without your family and friends.

Visitor Advice

Early in the day is the ideal time to visit Disneyland Paris. Just before the park closes, rides can be enjoyed without crowds. So, before you go, be aware of the park hours at Disneyland Paris.

Popular and packed attractions include Phantom Manor, Big Thunder Mountain, Star Wars attractions, and Indiana Jones and the Temple of Peril. Through the Disneyland Paris app, you can reserve Premier Access to these attractions and select the times that work best for you.

It is advised to reserve a room at one of the Disneyland Paris hotels. In addition to getting Extra Magic Time before the regular opening hours and discounted park tickets, you need two to three days to thoroughly tour all of Disneyland Paris' parks and resorts.

By purchasing your tickets in advance, you can avoid the inconvenience of waiting in huge lines at the entry and have a better time at Disneyland Paris.

Make reservations at your chosen Disneyland Paris restaurants before traveling. This is crucial because reservations for tables can sometimes be made up to two months in advance.

When visiting Disneyland Paris with your child, parents can use the Rider Switch option, which allows them to alternate riding on adult rides without having to stand in line again.

Chapter 6: The Parks

Disneyland is a huge, wide location with numerous distinct locations. This section will break down the many areas of the park and what can be done in each one. It is easily walked over the course of around 30 minutes.

Disneyland Park

The largest of Disneyland Paris' two theme park sectors are called Disneyland Park, or Parc Disneyland in French. The 'pink castle' and other well-known attractions may be found in this area, which is the park's oldest section.

As of mid-November 2021, Sleeping Beauty's Castle is once again open for visitors after spending part of 2021 under refurbishment and hence covered by scaffolding.

Main Street USA is located in Disneyland Park, which is also a lovely place to visit. When you enter Disneyland Park, this is the first site you see. It is designed to replicate US communities from the early 20th century. There are restaurants and shops in this area of the park.

The Sleeping Beauty Castle is the focal point of the entire Disneyland park, which also includes areas to the north, east, south, and west.

The parade takes place on Main Street, USA. The four themed areas are Fantasyland, Frontierland, Discoveryland (known as Tomorrowland in California), and Adventureland, which primarily has rides for young children.

Walt Disney Studios Park

The Walt Disney Studios Park is the smaller and more recent of Disneyland's two theme park sections. You can discover Toy Story rides, Cars rides, and other rides in this area of the park that are connected to Walt Disney Studios films.

The Walt Disney Studios Park doesn't quite have the same sense of "magic" as the other sections in Disneyland Paris and feels a little bit older. Notable is the park's Marvel Rides section, which debuted in 2022 and has already been a hit with visitors.

A modest shopping center with gift shops, restaurants, and other entertainment options can be found outside the two parks. This is comparable to the theme parks in Disney Springs and Downtown Disney in the USA.

Chapter 7: What to Bring to Disneyland Paris

What to Bring and Wear at Disneyland Paris

Put On a Backpack
Make sure to bring a backpack if you wish to bring anything, such as an additional sweater in case it gets cold or food. To go on the rides, bring a rucksack that will fit in the seat at your feet.

If You Come in The Early Spring, Late Fall, Or Winter
The initial plan for the European location of Disneyland Paris was for it to be in a warmer climate to match the sites in the USA. This is one of the most bizarre facts about Disneyland Paris. However, given its closeness to so many millions of people, Paris finally won the bid.

As a result, you should be ready for all four seasons, whether you visit Paris in the late autumn, winter, or early spring. During these periods of the year, the weather can quickly change, and it's not uncommon to have both sunny days and rain in a single hour.

As a result, I urge you to dress in layers so that you can protect yourself from the weather as needed. A small umbrella that will fit in your backpack, a cap, and gloves round out the list of necessities.

Common Questions Regarding Visiting Disneyland Paris

Are Both Parks Accessible in a Single Day?

Yes. Walt Disney Studios Park and Disneyland Park can both be visited on the same day. They are only a short distance apart and immediately next to one another. You must enter the parks through their respective separate entrances in order to visit either one.

Having saying that, I would pick to visit Disneyland Park if I could only visit one park and had the time and money to do so.

The bigger and more traditional of the two parks, with a very "Disney" vibe, is this one. One park alone may easily be explored in its entirety in a single day, with all of the available performances and minor rides being enjoyed.

Is The Single Rider Option Available?

The single-rider option for rides at Disneyland Paris was unavailable because of current global events. However, single riders are once again accessible beginning in November 2021. Use the app to check whether single riders are operating on the day you arrive at the location.

For instance, when my friends and I went to Disneyland, we were unable to enter a single rider line for attractions like Big Thunder Mountain in Disneyland Park or Crush's Coaster in Walt Disney Studios Park.

Is FastPass Available?

You can no longer purchase FastPass to shorten ride wait times because it has been retired. The option to purchase Disney Premier Access is now available. Access can be purchased on a per-ride basis, with prices normally ranging between €5 and €15.

What Is the Current State of Disneyland Paris?

Although it is still advised, mask use is not currently required at the park. Starting in the fall of 2021, parades are back.

Character meet and greets started occurring again on April 1, 2022; thus, a trip to Disneyland Paris will be very similar to how it was before 2020.

Parade at Disneyland Paris

If you don't enjoy roller coasters, is it still worthwhile to go to Disneyland Paris?

Yes! When it comes to Disneyland Paris, there is something for everyone. everything from leisurely riverboat cruises to looping rollercoasters. I had a terrific day despite being a huge lover of severe and frightening rollercoasters.

Where else is near Disneyland Paris?

The most popular designer retailer in France, La Vallée Village, is just a short distance away by foot (or train or bus). La Vallée Village is a retail center with approximately 110 stores, many of which sell high-end French designer goods.

There are 'accessible' designers like Sandro, Maje, Levi's, and Guess, as well as upscale brands like Gucci, Balenciaga, Prada, and Burberry. The Bicester Village Shopping Collection Villages include La Vallée Village.

Tips for Disneyland Paris

There are some things to know before visiting Disneyland Paris if this is your first time. There were certain things I wish I had known earlier after only recently experiencing the park for the first time!

Buy your tickets beforehand
If you're thinking about visiting Disneyland, you should be aware that my top piece of advice would be to buy your tickets in advance.

Be willing to wait
You should be ready for a day of waiting, which is something I was unaware of before visiting Disneyland Paris.

Unless you buy Premier Access, which is priced per ride and can quickly run into thousands of dollars, you should be ready to wait anywhere from five minutes to more than two hours between rides.

If available, single-rider admission to rides may have a substantially quicker wait time if you don't mind leaving your companions behind and riding alone.

For instance, it would have taken our group 60 minutes to reach the Ratatouille ride. Since we were riding alone, our wait time was barely 25 minutes.

Put on some relaxed walking shoes.
You may frequently have to wait a long time to access some rides, like I just said. As a result, I advise wearing your coziest sneakers and avoiding wearing any shoes that might be uncomfortable throughout the day. I also walked around the site for more than 20,000 steps throughout my visit.

Utilize the Disney France app.
I was given some great advice for visiting Disneyland Paris, one of which was to download the app ahead of time.

The app displays a list of all the rides that are open right now, along with their wait times (ride closures can happen at any time during the day).

The downloadable map will also indicate which rides currently permit single riders (but it regrettably does not provide you with the single rider waiting times) and how long the wait will be for each ride.

You're not permitted to dress up.
The park does not permit costumed visitors over the age of 12. Fortunately, if you're inventive, you can still dress like your favorite characters. 'Disney Bounding' is the term for this.

The majority of stores in the parks also sell Disney ears, although you might be able to remove them for some rides. Wearers of Disney ears range in age.

There are special releases of Disney ears in addition to the traditional Minnie ears, and I particularly adore my purple glittery pair. I strongly advise getting a pair of ears to wear on your future Disney vacation, wherever that may be, if you're looking to buy a keepsake from your stay at Disneyland Paris.

Go to Disneyland Park Next
If you want to visit both theme parks on the same day, go to Walt Disney Studios Park first, then Disneyland Park. There is much to see and do at Disneyland Park, which closes considerably later.

Select the rides you want to experience.
You won't be able to ride all of the rides if you only have a day to spend at Disneyland Paris (and especially if you want to spend the day at both parks). Even if hearing this can be discouraging, it naturally provides you with a reason to visit Disneyland Paris again in the future.

Get everyone in your group to choose the rides they want to ride the most, then prioritize going to those rides first to give you time to line up and ride them.

Additionally, I would advise attempting to ride the busiest rides (like Ratatouille and Space Mountain) early in the day since these are the ones with the longest waits.

Avoid going during public holidays.
I would advise avoiding French holidays if you want to visit Disneyland Paris and have the best chance of avoiding lengthy lines for each attraction. Since Disneyland Paris is so accessible from the UK, I would also advise staying away from UK bank holidays. Avoid weekends as well, if you can!

Parking is pricey.
Motorbikes cost €20, and parking at Disneyland Paris is €30. As a result, using public transportation to the park is probably a much simpler and less stressful choice if you are able to do so.

Disneyland Paris's closest train station is Marne-la-Valée-Chessy, which is about a two-minute walk from the park's entrance. With a direct connection to central Paris in around 45 minutes, the station is on the RER A.

Bring your own snacks and food.
I'm not the first to state that the food at Disneyland Paris isn't of the highest quality. When it comes to dining at DLP, there are two possibilities. The first option is to eat in a restaurant (get a table in advance as availability can fill up quickly), but this will cost you at least €30 per person.

The alternative is to get meals to go from one of the several fast food restaurants, stalls, or vans located throughout the park. However, most of these choices are expensive and unhealthy, with a hot dog costing €10. Every restaurant offers at least one vegetarian dish.

You can carry your own food and drink inside the park, but alcohol is not permitted, which is one of the most important travel advices for Disneyland that first-timers frequently forget. Even though people don't particularly enjoy picnics, you could still bring food into the park with you, which is what we did.

You don't have to be fluent in French
You don't need to speak French because Disneyland is such a popular worldwide tourist destination. Both parks' signage and attractions are bilingual, providing information in both French and English. Additionally, all employees are fluent in English.

Chapter 8: Lost at Disney!

Whether it's the main part of Walt Disney World, Hollywood Studios, or Discovery Island, the sheer thought of a kid being lost there is horrifying. Both security personnel and the cast are well-trained. The parent, however, plays a crucial part in the Disney World solution.

What to Do at Disney if Your Child Gets Lost

It takes quick thinking to know what to do if your youngster gets lost at Disney, and planning ahead makes it simpler. A parent's account of how they dealt with having their child misplaced at Disney offered guidance based on first-hand knowledge.

These procedures outline precisely what to do if your child gets lost at any Disney theme park, so you can return to experiencing the magic safely. This will help you stay prepared.

1. Prepare and inform beforehand
The guest at the Disney Resort claimed that the entire incident lasted only 10 or 15 minutes, but it was horrifying. The difference between a misplaced object and a missing child is stark. If you're going to Walt Disney World with a group, make sure there is a visible muster point.

Knowing how large Walt Disney World Resorts are is helpful. Splitting up may occur when some depart for Star Wars while others go to Indiana Jones.

Before the trip, whether it's to Animal Kingdom or another theme park, make sure children understand when to hold hands, when to stay by your side, and when to listen to their parents.

2. Take pictures
Useful knowledge is power. Work on helping your little Walt Disney World Resort visitor remember contact information. Additionally, make sure they are written down and with them at all times (particularly if the child is a young one).

Take a minute to take a picture when you go to the Magic Kingdom or Small World. This serves two purposes: it preserves the memories of the Disney Park visit and gives you quick access to a photo of your child from their stay at the Walt Disney World Resort.

3. Be prompt and composed.
Planning is important, and the Walt Disney Company has many safeguards in place to keep children safe. However, the decision to take quick action when a child goes missing in a Disney Park ultimately rests with the parents.

Control your breathing and maintain your composure by recalling your contingency plan in case of a Disney Park emergency. Get support. You have the option to calmly call their name and conduct a visual search. The former is preferable because it enables you to locate a cast member—if not your child—at least.

4. Quickly involve the staff
Speak out if you notice anything at a Walt Disney World resort. That entails locating the nearby Disney Park employee and telling them of the circumstances. The qualified employees at the Disney Resort can then follow internal procedures to return your child to you. The images are very helpful in this situation.

5. Adopt modern technology
Technology may be a buddy, whether you have an infant who might become lost or a young teen who wishes to go to Magic Kingdom or a theme park attraction alone. It may be a component of the overall strategy you develop to avoid the whole lost child problem.

There are many ways to find a misplaced youngster, from temporary phones to watches with monitoring features. They don't have to be long-term, but it seems like giving up privacy for security may be worth it to save a youngster if they get lost in Hollywood Studios or the Magic Kingdom.

6. Be watchful.
This is possibly the most important method for navigating Walt Disney Company properties safely. In any Disney Park, it's crucial to maintain caution despite the throng and magic.

Yes, you can ask any cast member or member of the Walt Disney Company for assistance. But the caregiver bears the main obligation. Therefore, the greatest method to provide safety through prevention, whether traveling domestically or internationally, is to be aware of your child and make appropriate travel plans.

Chapter 9: How to Take Great Photos at Disneyland Paris

In addition to being one of the world's most wonderful locations, Disneyland is also one of the most photographed. The Disney Parks consistently rank at the top of lists of the most Instagrammed locations in the world, and for good reason—they are incredibly stunning! Disneyland photography requires a particular level of skill because to the strong light, crowds of colorfully attired people, and the inevitable sticky, sweaty look everyone gets around 4 o'clock. Okay, perhaps not art. rather than craft. Craft AND art.

The idea is that photographing Disneyland is difficult. There's a good reason why Disney pays a bunch of photographers to set up shop at the top Disneyland photo locations and charge you a premium for their excellent work. However, even if you're not a pro, you can still shoot some seriously Instagram-worthy images of Disneyland. No matter your level of experience, our Disneyland image suggestions will help you capture your vacation like a pro, and our Disneyland photography advice will cover technique and style.

It is called the most wonderful spot on earth for a reason. A Disney theme park visit is often a once-in-a-lifetime opportunity for many of us. To be able to repeatedly recreate the event, you'll want your images to capture the magic you experienced during your stay. We've selected the top 24 Disney photo suggestions from seasoned photographers and Disney specialists, whether you're taking pictures, films, or both.

Consider Timing.
1. Disney is fantastic all year long.
Our trip took place in July, when there were the most visitors, and we spent the majority of our time in the parks in the middle of the day. Make the most of your visit whenever it is. Sometimes all you

can do is wait patiently or try your luck. People may pay more attention to you if you use a large camera, and they'll avoid you more often than if you only use a smartphone camera.

2. Be on time.
Try to get into the park before it opens to regular visitors for one of my favorite Disney photo suggestions. You will not only be able to take pictures with less people in the backdrop, but the morning light will also be softer. If getting in early isn't an option, be the first people inside when the rope drops for everyone and get to where you want to shoot right away.

3. Avoid battling the masses.
It goes without saying that you will have a lot of strangers in your photos if you visit a theme park in the height of the season. Try to enjoy the crowds and use them as a storytelling aspect rather than panicking and looking urgently for a place to put your family.

4. Keep your camera close by when you're idle.
When people are about to meet the characters or watch the parade, most photographers have their cameras ready, but during the less exciting times, they usually store them away. While I wait for the good stuff, I take some of my favorite photos.

5. Any light will function.
Finding great light is never easy when shooting at Disney (or any theme park, really). There is frequently both too little and too much light. But if you use a little light skillfully, you can get a fantastic Disney picture and keep it forever.

6. Take night-time photos.
Consider saving the kiddie attractions for the evening when the crowds are smaller as a theme park photography tip. Families with younger kids often head to Fantasyland at Disney World early in the day when the kids are still fresh, but going during golden hour will result in great light and fewer crowds.

Take Advantage of Angles.
7. To reduce the crowd, use imaginative angles.
Disney images without people in the background may seem impossible, but with some inventive angle-hunting, you can make it happen. Try to locate a location, such as on a bridge or up against a railing, where people will not be able to enter the backdrop of your image when taking important photos like Cinderella's Castle.

8. Use a wide-angle lens to capture the essence of your Disney vacation.
Theme parks are typically highly crowded. To avoid having to move too far away from your loved ones to acquire your photographs, I advise selecting a wide-angle lens. Additionally, a wider lens enables you to catch more of the surroundings and background, so you can fully convey your location. My 15mm fisheye lens is my absolute favorite to use at the Disney theme parks. Even while riding the coasters, I can use it to take pictures while sitting close to my subject and having my camera strap around my neck. The amusing aspect of distortion added by a fisheye or very wide-angle lens is perfect for photos taken at theme parks.

9. Aim both up and down.
Think carefully before framing. Don't be scared to position yourself in odd ways to obtain the shot. Since my children are small, I can easily get over them and use the ground as a crisp background. Lookups are also beneficial. I'm constantly considering how things would appear to a toddler. I continue to be intrigued and scan the area. Cleaning up your frame is made easy by looking up, down, or utilizing the foreground.

Take numerous detailed photos. I approach my subjects extremely closely. By isolating the subject from any distracting details, the frame is filled with what's important. Learn what your lens's minimum focusing distance is. I suggest a zoom lens with macro capabilities (a minimum focusing distance of 12 inches).

10. Photograph the Disney setting.
The story will be enhanced by pictures of friends, family, and characters, as well as by scenes from Disney World. Landscape pictures of the attractions and buildings can aid in setting the scene and creating a playful atmosphere. Try snapping pictures of Main Street, Cinderella's Castle, stores, or rides at Disney World. For these kinds of Disney pictures, you might want to use a narrower aperture so the depth of field is greater.

Utilize your Disney photos creatively.
11. Play around with various shutter speeds.
To avoid fuzzy photos and record the action, you should often use a quick shutter speed. However, I occasionally enjoy experimenting with slow shutter speeds to capture movement. Most theme parks do not permit the use of tripods; therefore, to prevent camera wobble, place the camera on a bench or fence. You can also try panning, which involves using a slow shutter speed to follow the subject while keeping the background blurry. For panning shots, I've discovered that a shutter speed of 1/15 to 1/50 of a second is ideal. It also helps to use high-speed burst mode and to press the shutter button repeatedly to take numerous pictures (I select my favorite photos and discard the rest).

12. Don't be hesitant to take careful pictures when riding.
The most sincere grins and interactions occur on rides. Always, the final pictures are my favorites. Just keep in mind to prioritize safety. Before taking any images, make sure your camera is absolutely safe.

Concentrate on the essentials.
13. Enter the picture.
As photographers, frequently find themselves in the background. Remember that you were also there. Sometimes it's crucial for your kids and family to see you in pictures. Try giving the camera to a family member or acquaintance you can trust to shoot a few pictures (you can set the camera up beforehand). You may also try taking a couple Disney selfies for fun. You can turn the camera around and

utilize live-view to see what you're filming if the LCD screen on some cameras flips out. Making sure your camera is set to focus when the shutter button is touched can prevent you from getting a shot with the camera turned around if you use rear-button focus. Keep your equipment secure if you plan to attempt to snap pictures while riding. I hold the camera strap firmly at all times, wrapping it around my arm or neck.

14. Concentrate on outcomes.
The animatronics may lure you to snap a hundred photos, but I promise they won't become your favorites. When the music and the motion are removed, they just lack vitality. You'll want to recall the experience more than the specifics of the attraction. Instead, pay attention to how your family is reacting. In ten years, these Disney images will resonate a lot more with you than a photograph of a statue or a safari animal.

15. Lay down the camera.
Putting the camera down and focusing on your family is one of the most crucial Disney photography tips. This one is incredibly difficult for me, but it's crucial. You might want to think about leaving the expensive camera in the hotel for one of the days if you plan to spend more than one day at the parks. Alternately, take the picture and then put the camera in your bag. Try to keep in mind the purpose of your visit: to create memories and enjoy yourself with your loved ones.

16. Keep in mind your goal.
Above all, keep in mind the original purpose of your shooting. Don't aggravate your family just to get a chance. It's vacation time now!
You won't get the genuine, joyful sensations you are seeking if it feels more like a Disney photo or video production than family fun. If a 5-minute movie or a photo book of every little detail makes you or your family exhausted, it is preferable to have a brief, excellent video or a few jaw dropping pictures. Keep it entertaining and fun!

Take photos of the Disney-specific items.
17. Take pictures of the Disney-themed cuisine.
Don't forget to take pictures of the sweets! It only makes sense to include some images of the kids enjoying the refreshments, as they are one of the nicest parts of visiting a park. It helps that it may be used as a bribe for kids who might need one, and it's a terrific way to end a lesson!

18. Take pictures of those distinctive Disney silhouettes.
Every time my family goes to Disney, I make sure to get pictures of my kids wearing their Mickey Mouse ears. When my eldest child was about two years old, I started taking silhouette photos of my kids wearing their Mickey ears to highlight the ears and illustrate how tiny they were. Look for locations with a bright background to take these kinds of pictures. The possibilities are unlimited because the hotels, restaurants, and shops all have distinctive interior designs.

Making A Memorable Disney Video with Your Family.

Even in sweltering heat and amid a throng of people, you can produce stunning, uncluttered videos of your Disney vacation. Despite the crowds, record-breaking heat, heavy equipment and young children, I managed to take a video of our journey to Disneyland Paris. Although it seems like a challenging scenario to film in, I'm pleased to offer some helpful Disney video advice.

19. The required equipment is minimal.
Only a camera, a strap, and a Canon EF 24-70mm f/2.8L II USM lens were all I had with me. A strap is all you need to use a variety of handheld stabilization techniques, although it does take some getting used to.

20. Consider the camera settings carefully.
Focus is manual while using your DSLR to record video. That implies that using a small aperture makes it challenging to achieve sharp focus. One method to get a nice bokeh and blurry background is to use a low f-stop. Moving really close to your subject is another way to get bokeh, even at f/4 or f/8. Putting a lot of space between your subject and your background is a third approach to achieving bokeh in addition to using a shallow aperture and getting close.

I advise using an outdoor aperture of f/4 to f/8 or greater. Since it's already challenging to view your LCD screen outside, doing this will help retain highlights and color and make manual focus more forgiving. Your chances of maintaining focus as your subject moves are better with a narrower aperture since it gives you a greater depth of field in which your subject may be in focus.

21. Keep in mind the principles of lighting and composition.
Despite the fact that video is mostly about motion, composition and lighting guidelines still apply. Always keep your shot in mind when searching for light and composing. Never forget to get up close to document facial expressions and feelings!

22. Make the most of the light that Disney has to offer.
There will always be light available when you visit the parks, regardless of the time. Even in bright light, you can choose dramatic lighting or find shade. When filming in the middle of the day, keep an eye out for gorgeous sun flickers caused by motion and shadows. I didn't use any filters, but you could if you wanted to increase your dynamic range in bright sunlight.

23. You can take stills from your Disney Video
For those of you who are shooting both photographs and videos, a brief but crucial tip You can extract stills from your videos as well, but bear in mind that they will be at the video's resolution, which is typically 1080p (1920 × 1080 pixels). With this resolution, I've never had any issues printing documents up to 5 by 7.

As opposed to still images, which typically have a 3:2 aspect ratio, videos have a 16:9 aspect ratio, so you will also need to crop the sides.

Be prepared!
Using a clear filter in place of a lens cover to be ready to shoot quickly while still protecting your lens is one of my favorite Disney photography tips.

Tips for Disney Videos

Don't only take pictures at Magic Kingdom.
Though the Magic Kingdom is undoubtedly magical, there are many other picturesque locations on the Disney premises. Listed here are some of our favorites:

- Disney's BoardWalk, Walt Disney World
- Disney Springs, Walt Disney World
- Downtown Disney District, Disneyland
- Outside the gates of Magic Kingdom, Walt Disney World

Chapter 10: Disneyland for Young Children

1. Before you travel, read Disney books or watch Disney movies. Most children won't find this challenging, but one of my favorite aspects of taking young children to Disney World was their excitement at seeing their favorite characters. Toddlers can be prepared for their first trip by reading Disney books, watching Disney movies, or even just tuning into Disney Junior.

It is very exciting to meet well-known figures and see Disney through their eyes when they encounter real-life Mickey Mouse, Disney Princesses, Buzz Lightyear, and other characters. Before visiting Disney World, a fantastic way to get children enthusiastic is to read books and watch Disney movies and cartoons like Toy Story.

Don't overlook the Disney Junior characters, either. Toddlers may meet their favorite characters, including Doc McStuffins, Vampirina, and Mickey Mouse, at the Disney Junior Dance Party in Disney's Hollywood studios. Kids can release excess energy by watching the Disney Junior Dance Party, which features their favorite Disney characters.

Activities for Toddlers at Disney World!
2. Toddlers Can Enjoy So Many Attractions
A toddler will have a blast at Disney parks because there are so many activities they may take part in! Over 100 attractions at Disney World don't have a height restriction.

My suggestions can be found by looking at the top toddler rides at each of the Disney World parks. However, even infants can ride! The Magic Kingdom park often has the most kiddie rides; however, there are also kiddie rides in Animal Kingdom, Epcot, and Disney's Hollywood Studios.

For the majority of the rides, there is no minimum height limit for infants and toddlers to ride on laps. Pirates of the Caribbean is one of them. However, youngsters won't soon forget riding the Alien Saucer ride (which has alien spinning saucers), aiming at Toy Story Mania, or seeing Woody in Toy Story Land! Even if some of the rides are too high for toddlers to experience, they will still enjoy the Toy Story Land sights and characters.

When we took my toddler son, he adored hugging all of his favorite Disney characters. Even though it wasn't his first time, the experience was just as spectacular.

While several have no minimum height requirements, some, like Slinky Dog Dash, do. Before you embark on your next adventure, make sure your children are tall enough.

3. While standing in line, toddlers might be amused.
While waiting in line for some of the rides, toddler-sized entertainment is available. Dumbo the Flying Elephant, which has a complete indoor play area, and The Many Adventures of Winnie the Pooh are two of my favorites for this in Magic Kingdom. My kids adored riding the Dumbo the Flying Elephant attraction and seeing the Winnie the Pooh characters.

This is why I adore taking toddlers to Disney World. Disney considers everything.

The entire Toy Story Land area at Disney's Hollywood Studios is a tremendous hit! In addition to feeling like toys in Andy's room or backyard, this area also has rides that are appropriate for young children. Additionally, Buzz Lightyear and Woody are frequently there for photo ops!

Kids can have fun in this indoor play area while waiting to ride Dumbo the Flying Elephant.

4. You can have fun without going to the parks.
Do not undervalue the effectiveness of the resort's transportation system if you are traveling to Walt Disney World Parks with a child in tow! When in doubt, toddlers can always enjoy a trip on the monorail, one of the transportation boats, the Disney Skyliner, or the bus.

Because Disney Magic permeates every nook and cranny of the resort, including the transportation, my kids were unaware that these weren't "rides." When you take young children to Disney World, they can enjoy themselves simply by riding the monorail, Disney Skyliner, buses, or boats throughout the theme park.

5. If at all possible, stay at a Disney hotel.
People occasionally ask me if they should stay locally or on-site at a Disney hotel.

I always advocate booking a room at a Disney Resort hotel because of all the advantages. However, staying on the property makes things so much easier, particularly if you are traveling to Disney World with little children.

It enables you to go back to the hotel for rest periods and naps. Additionally, there are activities for babies and toddlers to engage in, pools, and entertainment at Disney Hotels.

And a Disney vacation guarantees that your child will be immersed in the magic. Each of the individually themed hotels takes you to a completely different world, thanks to the theming and storytelling that permeate every inch of every Disney Resort hotel. When you stay on the resort, toddlers are showered with pixie dust from the moment they wake up until the moment they go to bed.

There are many hotels and locations to pick from, including Disney's Caribbean Beach Resort and Disney's Contemporary Resort, the only resorts where you can walk to and from the Magic Kingdom.

Each Disney Resort Hotel has a distinctive concept and is a stand-alone adventure!

6. Deliveries of groceries are available!
The majority of Disney Resort hotels let guests order groceries online and have them delivered right to their rooms. This is especially useful if you're taking children to Walt Disney World because you might need baby food, diapers, and toddler and baby snacks.

Take into consideration having these products brought to your accommodation if you are visiting Disney World with young children.

In order to make meal and snack times with toddlers easier, groceries can be delivered to your Disney Resort hotel.

7. Benefit from Early Theme Park Entry!
For several theme parks, you can enter the park earlier if you are staying at a Disney hotel. Use it if so! Because toddlers awaken early, you can enter the park before visitors with day tickets and get a head start on some of the rides.

Plan ahead and utilize Disney Genie Plus and Lightning Lanes (if applicable) for some of the most well-known rides. Additionally, make use of the new Disney Genie Service if you take young children to Disney World in 2023.

To make sure you fill your bucket, it is advisable to ride anything your child has their little heart set on first, and then move on to other rides you might regret missing. You won't have as much of an experience if you go during a busy time of year (holidays, spring break), compared to when it's less busy.

For younger visitors, Dumbo the Flying Elephant is a fantastic attraction.

8. Bring a stroller or rent one, but be mindful of the size of the stroller.

You can bring your own stroller to Walt Disney World, and because there is so much walking there, I strongly advise you to do so if you are taking kids. The parks are huge, and those tiny feet simply cannot keep up with all the trotting.

Additionally, youngsters can take a nap or an afternoon rest there. When visiting Disney World with young children, be sure to bring the stroller.

If you don't want to bring your own, Walt Disney World offers single and double strollers for hire that can accommodate children up to about age five. They are popular because they are easy to manoeuvre around parks. If you require one, check with guest services when you arrive.

There are specific stroller parking spaces close to the majority of the attractions (notice that theme parks now only allow strollers that are less than 31 inches wide and 52 inches long).

9. At Disney World, there are lots of facilities for infants and toddlers!

Disney naturally considers everything! Baby Care Centers were developed since they are one of the most family-friendly vacation destinations in the world, and they want children (and their parents) to have everything they need.

Each Disney World park provides a Baby Care Center with changing tables, nursing rooms, and products you can buy if you need diapers, baby food, etc. if your toddler or baby needs a break.

Each baby care center also serves children of all ages. You can find a calm, pleasant area to relax in. Additionally, some places feature potties that are toddler-sized if your little buddy is potty training!

That is definitely kid-friendly! One of the best locations for your family to unwind is a baby care center.

If your child requires acetaminophen or other over-the-counter medication, there are also first aid stations available. Both high chairs and changing tables are available in public restrooms.

10. There Are Many Snacks for Toddlers!
What would toddler life be like without snacks? If you're taking little children to Disney World, carry snacks. However, if you don't or don't have enough, rest assured that Walt Disney World has you covered on this front.

In the parks and resort gift stores, some of my kids' favorite snacks were offered—but only with the special Disney pixie dust!

I mean goldfish-style crackers shaped like Mickey ears. They obviously taste better. The flavor of the Mickey-shaped pretzels is undoubtedly better. Veggie chips molded to resemble Mickey Mouse's head? The vitamins are even tasteless. I completely forgot to mention the Mickey-shaped churros, soft pretzels, and ice cream!

During your trip to Disney World, your toddler won't go hungry! Naturally, every restaurant and fast-food establishment also offers kid-friendly menus.

11. Book character dinners or breakfasts early!
Make reservations for meals in advance, especially for character breakfasts or dinners. These get booked up fast! For your child, you won't need to make reservations at parks, but you will need to do so at restaurants.

Check all the character breakfast options, including this one at Topolino's Terrace, to see who will be there and what will be served. Toddlers love character breakfasts, dinners, and character meals because they can interact directly with their favorite characters without having to wait in a long line at the parks.

All guests can currently make advance dining reservations 60 days in advance.

At Walt Disney World Resort character lunches, kids like spotting their favorite characters.

12. You may also ride the attractions you desire!
The Rider Switch option is also available at Walt Disney World, and I strongly advise using it once or twice if you are traveling there with little children.

Rider Switch allows you to enjoy rides with height limits that are not suitable for young children, such as Space Mountain in Magic Kingdom Park, Tower of Terror in Hollywood Studios, and Expedition Everest in Animal Kingdom.

If there is another adult in your group traveling to Disney, they should stay with the non-rider while the other takes advantage of the attraction. Then you trade places so that the returning adult stays with the child or baby and the other adult may enjoy the attraction without having to wait in the starting line when the first adult returns.

It's a terrific idea for one adult to keep the kids occupied while the other enjoys the attraction, and then switch, using Rider Switch.

13. In-room childcare is a service provided by Disney at its resort hotels.
You can arrange for in-room childcare if you and your partner or other adult family members want to enjoy a romantic supper or the park's nighttime fireworks. The Walt Disney Company collaborates with Kids-Night-Out to offer on site childcare in your hotel room

Due to the epidemic, this was temporarily discontinued. Check again at your hotel to see if this has continued.

14. Park Entry is Free for Children Under Two!
One of the selling aspects is this. The Disney theme parks DO NOT REQUIRE PARKING TICKETS FOR CHILDREN UNDER TWO! You no longer need to worry if they sleep, need a break, or don't enjoy every moment, thanks to this. Another good reason to take young children to Disney World.

15. A Park at a Time, Please!
People frequently ask me which Disney park is ideal for toddlers when they are organizing a trip to the theme parks. There are attractions for toddlers in each of the Disney parks, though Magic Kingdom DOES have the most alternatives for them, including "It's a small world," "Under the Sea - Journey of the Little Mermaid," and "Peter Pan's Flight" (my favorite).

Epcot boasts a walkable floor plan, an aquarium, and kid-friendly rides including Frozen Ever After and Seas with Nemo and Friends. Additionally, the World Showcase is a great attraction for kids because it is highly kid-friendly. Kids can obtain a card about that nation from the Cast Member at each "Kidcot" stop, which is located in each country. They can exit and stretch their legs as they enter a foreign country.

Wild animals and kid-friendly rides can be found at the Animal Kingdom. There are numerous places to stroll, a large dinosaur playground area, and a carnival area. Additionally, there are unusual elements like monkeys in the trees, and my kids really enjoy the Kilimanjaro Safari.

African creatures are also on display at Disney's Animal Kingdom, including:
- Africa Elephants
- Hogs
- Birds
- Lions

Plus, more. All the animals in Disney's Animal Kingdom were adored by our youngsters. Additionally, your kids will enjoy the Festival of the Lion King and the Finding Nemo attraction at the Animal Kingdom if they enjoy the Lion King and Finding Nemo.

Additionally, you shouldn't skip seeing the Animal Kingdom at night when it is beautifully illuminated up.

Along with Toy Story Land, Star Wars, a show with the Muppets, Lightning McQueen, Mickey and Minnie's Runaway Coaster, and so much more, Hollywood Studios includes several themed restaurants.

Kids will enjoy a lot of the entertaining attractions at Disney's Hollywood Studios. However, keep in mind that Hollywood Studies has the least number of kid-friendly attractions. Even yet, the vibrant colors and sights of Hollywood Studios can fascinate young kids merely by wandering around with them.

There are many entertaining attractions and rides at the Magic Kingdom. The Country Bear Jamboree at Magic Kingdom is a favorite among our kids. On their journey to their subsequent adventure, the Disney Adventure Friends Calvacade also marches through the local streets.

Everyone adores the view of the Magic Kingdom's Beacons of Magic, where enchanted fairy lights and twinkles illuminate numerous structures. Not to be overlooked is Disney Enchantment, a display of fireworks that illuminates the Magic Kingdom skyline.

However, if you are traveling to Disney World with toddlers, visiting one park at a time is definitely easier on them and you to get the most out of your trip.

This allows you to experience more of each park, including parades and performances like the Celebration of the Festival of the Lion King. Additionally, you won't feel as like you are missing out on time at another park if you need to take an afternoon break.

16. Unwind—this is Disney!

My son may or may not have had an accident on the floor of one of the parks at Disney when he was learning to use the toilet. The problem is this.

Disney is the one place where your kid can let loose and be anything they want to be: joyful, unhappy, angry, throw up, laugh uncontrollably, and make noise. The kid in all of us and children alike will like this area.

If your child has a "toddler moment" anywhere on the Disney World property, don't worry about it. They may be overstimulated, the days may be long, and it may be hot. It's alright. However, they will generally have a great time.

Questions and Answers

Can a 2-year-old have fun in Disney World?

Absolutely! A 2-year-old will have a blast at Disney World! This age group will enjoy a wide variety of activities, including rides, Disney Junior characters, character breakfasts, balloons, and so much more.

We took our 2-year-olds to Disney several times when they were toddlers, and each trip was a fantastic, magical experience. Even using the boat or the monorail at Disney World can be enjoyable and joyous for a two-year-old, however they might need to work on shorter days. The Magic Kingdom and Animal Kingdom will also be favorites.

Where in Disney World Should Toddlers Spend Their Time?

But at Walt Disney World, I would suggest Magic Kingdom and Animal Kingdom for children. If you ask me which Disney World park is the greatest for toddlers, my answer is "all of them."

Actually, Epcot is the finest place to travel with a stroller because the walking spaces are larger and because children can nap while parents explore some of the World Showcase. We have taken many peaceful strolls throughout Epcot. And Epcot does have rides suitable for young children.

However, Magic Kingdom will provide the most entertainment for a two-year-old and the entire family in terms of characters, parades, and the majority of rides. Animal Kingdom, which has multiple kid-friendly attractions and features creatures that toddlers like, would come in second place. Rafiki's Planet Watch in Animal Kingdom also houses a petting zoo.

How Can a Disney Vacation Be Arranged with A Toddler?

For convenience and kid-friendliness, I highly suggest making reservations at one of the Disney Resort hotels on-site!

Once your accommodation is reserved, open the Disncy app, choose your theme park tickets, make your reservations (needed till 2023). Next, book your character breakfast and advanced dining reservations as soon as you can, 60 days out.

If you are staying at one of the Disney Resort hotels, I also suggest taking use of toddlers' early rise and shine to take advantage of Early

Entry so you may enter the parks early and ride as much as you can before the crowds arrive.

Last but not least, get comfortable with the new Disney Genie on the My Disney Experience app (add your preferences so it can work for you), and if you like, buy any Disney Genie+ or Lightning Lane add-ons before or on the day of your theme park visit. Then, have fun!

Are Toddlers Allowed to Visit Disney World?

Yes, young children and infants CAN and SHOULD visit Disney World. A 3-year-old and a 103-year-old may enjoy Disney together!

Disney World, keep in mind, grows with your child. Each stage of life and age is unique. It is impossible to stress how fantastic it is for your young children to see their favorite Disney characters or princesses and how happy your toddler looks when they see them and embrace them. For all ages, but especially for young children, it is a beautiful and extremely special experience!

Watch the excitement in your child's eyes as they take in the Magic Kingdom's fireworks or Beacons of Light. They will be enthralled!

Chapter 11: Disneyland for Adults

It's possible that you believe Disneyland is solely for children, but this couldn't be further from the truth, and I'm here to convince you that Disneyland is actually way cooler for adults!

I had the good fortune to visit Disneyland frequently while growing up. Even as an adult, I continue to attend Disneyland; in fact, after moving to Orange County, I finally gave in and got a Magic Key.

Even though I've always loved going to Disneyland, I almost think I do now that I'm older! Adults can enjoy a wide range of activities at Disneyland, including rides, shows (both action-packed and more laid-back), seasonal festivals, lots of photo opportunities, and the best part: eating and drinking (including alcoholic beverages).

Disneyland offers everything from Instagrammable snacks to ethnic fusion cuisine, inventive cocktails, and even fine dining establishments. You could almost argue that Disneyland is a gourmet destination. This is why I, like with many other adults visiting Disneyland, enjoy eating and drinking my way through the parks.

Additionally, even as an adult, one may still experience a sense of wonder and nostalgia. I know Disney tends to misuse the word "magical," but it's still very magical.

If you're wondering if going to Disneyland as an adult is enjoyable or even worthwhile, I'm here to say YES, 1000000%! And believe me, there are a lot more adults who concur from Disneyland.

Read this chapter if you're thinking of taking an adult trip to Disneyland as it will help you to learn how to do it right and have the best fun possible. I'm here to provide you advice on what to do, where to eat and drink, and all the insider insights you need to know, including the greatest adult rides at Disneyland.

The Top Disneyland Tips for Adults

Why would an adult go to Disneyland?
Because it's simply plain FUN, of course!

Walt Disney also wanted Disneyland to be a location where people of all ages could enjoy themselves. Today, the company still bases every choice on this concept.

You'll find something to adore at Disneyland as an adult, whether it be the roller coasters or the more laid-back attractions, the food (casual and fine dining), the drinks (both alcoholic and non-alcoholic), the performances, the shopping options, or anything else!

In addition, travelling as an adult gives you complete freedom! Would you like to ride each rollercoaster several times throughout the day? Do you want to overindulge on the treats and snacks? Would you like to see all the bars in California Adventure? Nobody is preventing you!

When Adults Should Visit Disneyland

The best time to visit Disneyland as an adult is to avoid weekends and school holidays, although this should go without saying.

This will result in fewer crowds, which will make your trip more enjoyable.

Thanksgiving week, the week before Christmas to New Year's, spring break (the week before Easter), the start of summer vacation (June), and fall break (the second week of October) are when it is most congested.

There is a modest increase in crowds around holidays, on Halloween, and during festivals (like the Food & Wine Festival), but it's not too awful unless you go on the weekend or during school breaks or holidays.

In general, January and February are the least crowded months to visit Disneyland. You'll encounter the fewest crowds in the weeks after the conclusion of the holiday celebrations. However, keep in mind that during this time, the parks close earlier and several attractions close to undergo renovations, so you might not have the best experience.

Checking out the Magic Key permit holders' access calendar is one useful technique to anticipate crowds. The dates that are reserved for pass holders are often the busiest; however, the dates reserved for the most costly passes will be EXTRA wild!

The least congested times of the day are typically in the mornings, especially immediately following rope drop. The wait times are significantly more tolerable during this time, especially for the more well-liked rides. Additionally, I've noticed that it becomes quieter later in the evening, about 9 o'clock.

Which amusement park, California Adventure or Disneyland, is more suitable for adults?

Visit both if at all possible because they are each great in their own way! You may maximize your enjoyment of your adult trip to the Disneyland Resort by going to both.

Simply put, Disneyland has more attractions and better rides. Adults can find greater food and beverage options at California Adventure, as well as more thrilling rides, not to mention booze.

I'd say that California Adventure, with its more upscale dining options, booze, more daring rides, generally draws more to adults. Due to the limited number of rides, I eventually become bored. I enjoy riding all the rides at Disneyland, but I usually get hungry and want something a little fancier to eat. I can enjoy the best of both worlds by going to both parks!

Consider what kind of experience is important to you if you can only visit one park.

What Should an Adult Bring to Disneyland?

I always walk at least 10 miles throughout a full day at Disneyland, so comfy shoes are essential! My friend typically wears the Tree Dashers (women / men), while I literally just wear Allbirds shoes when I visit parks. I wear the Wool Runners (women / men) and Tree Runners (women / men).

Power bank: Since you'll probably use the app all day, it's a good idea to keep a battery pack close by so you can recharge your devices.

Reusable Water Bottle: Fill up at the water fountains to save money instead of purchasing pricey bottles of water (you'll have more money for snacks and sweets).

Fun Disney-Themed Clothing: Show off your Disney spirit and embrace your mature self by wearing some Disney-themed shirts to the park!

Wear a jacket or sweater because it may be cold in the morning and warm in the midday depending on the time of year you visit. Bring a jacket with you in case it gets chilly! You can store it in a locker if you don't want to carry it around; my friend frequently does this and also carries a change of clothes.

Another way to show your Disney spirit is with mouse ears! There are a ton of adorable ones available on Etsy and from Disney (I've amassed quite the collection by this point).

Snap those beautiful Disney experiences with the camera! At Disneyland, I primarily use my phone to take pictures, but if you want something better, I recommend my Sony a6000, a lightweight camera that takes incredible pictures.

Sunscreen: Since you're visiting Disneyland as an adult, chances are the sun will be shining brightly. After all, this is So-Cal. You'll need to protect your skin even on cloudy days.

Sunglasses: It gets BRIGHT out there! The worst sensation is when I forget my sunglasses and have to spend the entire day squinting into the light. Grab a pair of sunglasses right away!

Hand Sanitizer: I mean, the parks were crowded with filthy kids touching, well, everything even before the outbreak. Both parks have sanitizing stations scattered throughout them, but they are rarely functional, so bring your own.

The Best Adult Activities at Disneyland

One of the nicest areas of Disneyland for adults is Galaxy Edge, which is illuminated at night.

Adults may enjoy some of the top rides at Disneyland's Star Wars: Galaxy's Edge.

The Best Rides at Disneyland for Adults

Which rides at Disneyland are ideal for adults? It might be challenging to decide where to begin when there are so many Disney attractions, especially if you only have a limited amount of time to spend at the parks.

Of course, there are many rides that you enjoyed as a child that are ideal for evoking nostalgia (I can guarantee you that the majority of them are just as amazing today as they were then).

Alternately, you could ride all the thrilling coasters, but be aware that as an adult, they can affect you differently (helloooo whiplash). And when you need a break from the riskier rides, there are plenty available to keep you entertained.

Here are all the top adult rides at Disneyland, in whatever case.

Adults' Top Thrill Rides at Disneyland

Rise of the Resistance (Disneyland): The second ride at Star Wars: Galaxy Edge to launch, Rise of the Resistance is one of the park's newest attractions. It is one of the park's coolest and most creative attractions, and it is also incredibly immersive. Joining the Resistance as they engage the First Order in a titanic fight makes you feel truly a part of the narrative. Even if you don't consider yourself to be a huge Star Wars fan, I can assure you that you will adore this one!

I'll admit that Space Mountain at Disneyland feels a little stale now that I've been on Rise of the Resistance. To this day, it remains one of my all-time favorite rides, despite the fact that it was always one of my favorites as a child. You genuinely get the sensation of flying across space.

Big Thunder Mountain Railroad (Disneyland): Inspired by the hoodoos of Bryce Canyon, this roller coaster with a Western Gold Rush theme features beautiful scenery and lots of thrills. It's most exciting at night, in my opinion. Please be aware that certain parts are uneven.

I've always like the Indiana Jones Adventure at Disneyland because it inspires a sense of adventure. You travel in a jeep through the deep tunnels of the Temple of the Forbidden Eye, so it's not truly a roller coaster. This one has a lot of bumps and jerks; we make fun of the fact that they appear to become worse every time we ride it.

Matterhorn (Disneyland): Avoid the abominable snowman as you speed through a snow-covered summit in an alpine sled. If you have whiplash, you might want to avoid this one because it contains quick twists and is a little bumpy. Additionally, watching the fireworks is the greatest moment to take this. It's a lovely sight to see the castle and the It's a Small World front lit up over the holidays.

Incredicoaster (California Adventure): Incredicoaster, in my opinion, is one of the best Disneyland attractions for adults and the park's most underappreciated attraction. It's a traditional, fast roller coaster with a loop that is significantly more daring than the others in the parks. If any of it troubles you, skip this one because it contains a loop, high dips, and sharp curves. PS: It goes much faster at night.

California adventure game Radiator Springs Racers, which was inspired by Pixar's Cars, takes you on a voyage through the desert environment of the West in the company of lifelike animatronic cars and culminates in a significant race. I adore this one because of the breathtaking scenery; I definitely advise taking it around dusk! Due to the consistently long lineups and the fact that the Lightning Lane is not included with the regular Genie+, I also advise single riders for this one.

Mission: Breakout, a Guardians of the Galaxy episode! (California Adventure) Assist Rocket in freeing the other Guardians from the Collector's castle. This one is my favorite because it's not only exciting, but also just plain enjoyable! There are several free-falling drops on the ride. If you don't like the way it makes your stomach drop, skip this one. Another thing to keep in mind is that the line for this almost always takes longer than what it estimates.

Adults' Coolest Disneyland Rides

It's a Small World (Disneyland): I know this one could seem uninteresting to some, but it's a great opportunity to unwind and rest your feet because it lasts for 15 minutes. When it has the festive overlay, it is most definitely worth getting on!

Take a journey on the perilous rivers of the jungle on Disney's Jungle journey, where puns are common and animals rule. Although some guides are better than others, the jokes are usually funny, and the journey is leisurely and gorgeous. When I was younger, I found this one to be quite dull, but as an adult, I've grown to love it more—especially for the humor! Instead of doing this one at night, do it during the day when the guides are less likely to rush through it.

The longest ride in the parks, at 16 minutes, is Pirates of the Caribbean at Disneyland. You'll see Jack Sparrow make multiple appearances on the ride, which I appreciate that they've finally incorporated. The ride has two drops, and they are both larger than you may imagine. If sitting in the first two rows makes you uncomfortable because you might get wet, ask to be seated in the rear.

Take a boat ride through a charming fairytale land that includes tiny copies of the cottages, palaces, and villages seen in various Disney movies on the Storybook Land Canal Boats at Disneyland. Storybook Canal is fantastic and sadly underappreciated. Going during or after sunset is ideal because it is so magical and romantic.

Sit in a vibrant antique automobile as it "dances" about the Luigi's yard to Italian music with the help of Luigi's Rollickin' Roadsters. It's lovely and enjoyable to boot! Be aware that this ride has some spinning, though I don't think it's particularly harsh.

Go on an amazing hang-gliding journey around the world with Soarin' Around the World (California Adventure). featuring breathtaking IMAX projection, aerial photography, and even certain odors to make you feel like you're flying around the world! I adore this as a travel blogger! I will admit that I like the previous California version that they had; they do bring it back for the Food and Wine Festival, so if you chance to be planning your adult Disney vacation at that time, definitely go on it.

The Little Mermaid is a fantastic choice if you're searching for a calm ride that rarely has a long wait.

Chapter 12: Best Disneyland Paris Rides

Disneyland Paris's Crush's Coaster
The absolute finest ride in Disneyland Paris is Crush's Coaster! Which attractions should you prioritize if you only have a limited amount of riding time while visiting Disneyland Paris? While Disneyland Paris does include a few original rides, the majority of its other attractions may initially appear to be exact replicas of those seen at American theme parks.

Do not be misled; Disneyland Paris handles these rides uniquely, and they should be given first priority. Here are our family's top five Disneyland Paris attractions.

Crush's Coaster: The Finding Nemo-themed Crush's Coaster puts riders in a turtle shell that pivots as it travels along the track, allowing them to see movie sequences. Although it is a smooth ride without inversions, the darkness makes it somewhat intense. There are definitely some appropriate analogies to be made to Guardians of the Galaxy: Cosmic Rewind at Walt Disney World.

Big Thunder Mountain: Compared to the rides at Disneyland and Disney World, Big Thunder Mountain is more intense and has a more pleasant atmosphere.

Star Wars Hyperspace Mountain: Space Mountain on steroids with inversions (this is a true coaster, baby!) with the theme of Star Wars.

Phantom Manor: This is a French version of the Haunted Mansion with a whole different plot. Much macabre and creepier.

Pirates of the Caribbean: A fantastic experience with an immersive line and various new areas is Pirates of the Caribbean: Pirates at Disneyland Paris. It was difficult for us to determine whether we preferred this rendition somewhat more than the Disneyland original. However, it clearly goes beyond the scaled-back version of Pirates at Walt Disney World.

Chapter 13: How Many Days Should You Plan to Visit Disneyland Paris?

What amount of time do you need to budget if Disneyland Paris piques your interest? Our family spent three days in the parks, however the first and last days were only partial days due to prior travel arrangements.

Here is a general guideline to consider. In terms of scale and scope, I see Disneyland Paris as being about comparable to the Disneyland Resort in Anaheim, California. It has fewer rides (and a lesser second park), but it also has more hotels on-site than Disneyland and a relatively equal Downtown Disney area in Disney Village. Therefore, if you are the type of visitor who would spend three days at Disneyland, three days will likely be sufficient to fully experience Disneyland Paris.

However, if you're not a huge Disney fan and simply want a taste of the resort while on a European vacation that's more about seeing things outside of theme parks, a single day is definitely achievable. In that case, I would definitely completely forgo visiting Walt Disney Studios Park (or only travel there to ride Crush's Coaster with Premier Access before returning). If you've already been to a Disney park in the US or abroad, make the most of your experience by concentrating on what makes Disneyland Paris special. I'd make sure to have a very busy day for you and your children, beginning at park opening and going as late as you and they can.

In the end, I thought that in three days, I had seen and done about 90% of everything I had intended to. We went during a particularly hot period of the year, which required us to go a little more slowly than we otherwise would have. And in the midst of a really ambitious and cram-packed European journey, we visited Disneyland Paris.

Bonus Chapter: Disneyland Paris Itinerary

This one-day Disneyland Paris schedule includes suggestions for restaurants, performances we should see, and other fun elements as well as a step-by-step tour plan for maximizing rides. Our one-day agenda balances an effective sightseeing schedule with opportunities to take it easy and take in the "Disney Details" to create the ideal day for us in Disneyland Paris.

This is neither a "commando style" tour itinerary or a how-to manual for cramming as many attractions as you can into a limited amount of time at the expense of other activities. It's necessary to do a lot, but this schedule strikes a balance between quantity and quality. Efficiency is crucial, but since Disneyland Paris is the most elaborate and well-detailed Disneyland-style park in the world, you must take your time and truly enjoy everything this Disney park has to offer.

This advice makes a few assumptions, such as that you will go on a day that is moderately busy, that you will utilize Standby Passes appropriately (grab them whenever you can, not just when they are indicated in the plan), and that you will arrive at the park when it opens and remain until it closes. Because this is one of the rare parks where the majority of popular attractions use Standby Pass or Disney Premier Access, exploring Disneyland Paris efficiently is really easy. The Standby Pass should be adequate; we do not advise buying the latter unless you are traveling on a day that is exceptionally busy.

Also keep in mind that not all attractions are listed in detail in our 1-day Disneyland Paris itinerary. Instead, we build a touring schedule that can be completed in a single day by making value judgments about the top attractions

Let's look at how you ought to approach this perfect day...

Rise and Shine: For a first visit to any Disney resort, I strongly recommend staying on-site, and Paris is no exception. My recommendation is to stay in Sequoia Lodge, but if you have the money, I imagine the views from the Disneyland Hotel can't be beaten.

Aside from Extra Magic Hours, staying at a Disney hotel gives you access to Fantasyland and Discoveryland two hours before the park opens to the general public. I prefer to concentrate on taking pictures of a mostly deserted park during this period. However, at Disneyland Paris, you should always begin each day with...

It's Westward Ho! The most popular attraction at Disneyland Paris, Big Thunder Mountain Railroad, is a great way to start your day. Although you could always do this later using a Standby Pass, it is best to arrive as soon as possible in the morning.

After that, do a loop back into Fantasyland to finish up a number of those well-liked rides quickly.

Wonderful Morning - Any castle park in Fantasyland, including Disneyland Paris, is a great place to start the day, in my opinion. Like the rest, one of the main reasons to start here is the abundance of surrounding attractions, each of which can develop a brief wait, and those brief waits add up.

Peter Pan's Flight is a good place to start before moving on to the other dark attractions. (Take note that Storybook Land Canal Boats and Casey Jr. may start operating later than the rest of the park.) Finish with a stroll through Alice's Curious Labyrinth, and be sure to climb all the way to the top for spectacular views of Fantasyland.

There's Adventure Out There! According to the park map, you could believe that you can quickly finish this area by visiting Pirates of the Caribbean and Indiana Jones and the Temple of Doom. That is not true in the slightest. The Indiana Jones coaster is terrible, to start. It is a waste of time because it has no thematic elements and is brief. I bet you won't appreciate the meticulous attention to detail and stunning beauty of the park if you visit Disneyland Paris for this.

However, I know you won't skip this Pirates of the Caribbean ride, which is among the top Disney attractions in the world. The Swiss Family Treehouse and Skull Rock are two must-see attractions on Adventure Isle, so be sure to spend some time there. Le Passage Enchanté d'Aladdin, a charming little walk-through exhibit, is another underrated gem.

DRAGON! - Disneyland Paris is a contentious theme park that elicits a love-it-or-hate response from Disney devotees. People that despise Disneyland Paris did the park without any dragon time, which is what I have concluded from my extremely scientific research because I have never seen this kind of reaction to any other Disney park in the world.

As a result, as a quick mood booster, swing by to visit the dragon beneath the castle sometime in the morning. (If you make more stops during the day, your likelihood of enjoying the park will rise even more.) I can assure you that stopping to visit the dragon will leave you feeling energized and eager to explore the area. The finest part about waking up, according to the jingle, is seeing a dragon!

If Walt's - An American Restaurant is open, I highly recommend going there for lunch. If it is, try to make reservations early in the morning before visiting any sights. Blue Lagoon Restaurant is a table service option that might be open if it isn't. Although I don't like for either restaurant's food, both have fantastic atmospheres and are well worth a visit.

The jovial Toad Hall (a must-visit for Mr. Toad fans when it's actually open) or Cowboy Cookout BBQ are two options for counter service. These eateries rank among the greatest themed Disney theme park restaurants in the world.

Afternoon Exploration: You should have time to take it easy before and after the afternoon parade (for example, you could stop and look at the dragon around 17 more times). I can't emphasize enough how crucial discovery is in Disneyland Paris. It is a park that should be savored like a great wine since it is a veritable treasure trove of intricacies.

Despite its shortcomings, Disneyland Paris has a beautiful sense of romance and a design that successfully combines the otherwise opposed feelings of grandiosity and quaintness. It's a park for exploring, snapping pictures, and just taking in the essence of fantastic thematic design. Similar to Tokyo DisneySea, the park's general design seems to have been left up to the Imagineers.

You might see my remarks regarding the Indiana Jones ride above as satire, but I genuinely believe that there is a negative correlation between visitors' opinions of that ride and those of the park as a whole. The park at Disneyland Paris is not for thrill-seekers or ride junkies. It's for the kind of visitor who could spend all day exploring the World Showcase.

So it should come as no surprise that I suggest going here for a post-lunch coffee (so forgo dessert and coffee if you dine at Walt's). I have already extolled the delights of this tiny establishment on Main Street.

One of our favorite things to do when traveling to France is to start the day by stopping in a little boulangerie in the morning (or really any time of the day). Although it still feels European, it's ironic that this quaint and cozy bakery at Disneyland Paris is actually American. That doesn't take anything away from it, though.

73

Disney Stars on Parade is a daytime parade that was introduced last year to celebrate Disneyland Paris' 25th anniversary. It is highly recommended. It is time well spent thanks to the lovely costumes, creative floats, and upbeat music. Oh, and there's a fire-breathing dragon just underneath the castle, so that's a major plus!

You could probably safely avoid this if you're not a parade fan, but it's usually really simple to secure a nice place only 15 minutes in advance, so it's not like you're giving up much to see it. This is also an excellent time to attend one of the seasonal stage shows that are likely to be there, depending on what time of year you visit. To learn more, consult your daily time guide.

Thunder Mesa: "Disneyland Paris is the most beautiful park, but..." is a relatively typical one, often followed by reservations about upkeep, the caliber of the attractions, and the cast members (all of which can be valid to some extent). In Frontierland, also known as Thunder Mesa, none of these issues exist. This is Disneyland Paris operating at peak efficiency.

It was positioned here with the intention that you would see Thunder Mesa in the late afternoon light before sunset, which is a very wonderful experience for a Disney theme park enthusiast. Do Phantom Manor and Big Thunder Mountain Railroad via Standby Pass (if possible), pay a visit to Lucky Nugget Saloon for dinner (be aware of their closing times to avoid being forced to eat at the appalling Cafe Hyperion), and plan your day so that you can take a sunset cruise on the Thunder Mesa Riverboats.

Discovering the Night at Disneyland Paris made the correct decision to forgo the Tomorrowland idea in favor of a Discoveryland that was inspired by Jules Verne. It is essentially Tomorrowland, with a different name and some changes to the plot and specifics. It is best enjoyed at night, just like the other Tomorrowlands (who knew neon lighting was so common on Verne's day!). Les Mystères du Nautilus is a must-see attraction, despite the fact that many visitors disregard it because it's "only" a walkthrough.

My head actually hurt from the ride on Hyperspace Mountain, which is a Star Wars version of Space Mountain. But it's enjoyable and worth trying at least once. (Plus, I'm an old-timer and have witnessed younger people exit the attraction beaming widely, so perhaps it's just me.)

Disney Dreams, a fantastic nighttime castle display at Disneyland Paris, introduced the idea of a mixed-media castle performance, and this is its replacement. Disney Illuminations is still a must-see, even though it's not quite as good as its predecessor.

In addition to other things, it has fire, pyrotechnics, water fountains, lasers, and castle projections. A montage display that emphasizes French and other European Disney stories is bound together by Peter Pan. You must not miss this show since it has both passion and stunning technical prowess. For those who want to locate the ideal location and take pictures, we have this viewing and photography guide.

You'll see that we didn't spend much time on Main Street before this, despite the fact that it was the pinnacle of Main Street layouts. This is due to the fact that, following Disney Dreams, it is impossible to access other lands, although Main Street is still accessible for another 30 minutes or so for shopping and relaxing. Visit each of the arcades, look around the shops, and overall be in awe at the level of attention to detail that went into creating this version of Main Street, USA.

Regardless of the season you visit, you should be able to complete all of this at Disneyland Paris in a single day. Despite this, I personally could stay in Disneyland Paris for days on end and just take it all in.

Travel Journal: For Jotting Down Unforgettable Encounters

Disneyland Paris Travel Journal

Notes:

Disneyland Paris Travel Journal

Notes:

Disneyland Paris Travel Journal

Notes:

Disneyland Paris Travel Journal

Notes:

Disneyland Paris Travel Journal

Notes:

Disneyland Paris Travel Journal

Notes:

Disneyland Paris Travel Journal

Notes:

Disneyland Paris Travel Journal

Notes:

Disneyland Paris Travel Journal

Notes:

Disneyland Paris Travel Journal

Notes:

Disneyland Paris Travel Journal

Notes:

Disneyland Paris Travel Journal

Notes:

Disneyland Paris Travel Journal

Notes:

Disneyland Paris Travel Journal

Notes:

Disneyland Paris Travel Journal

Notes:

Disneyland Paris Travel Journal

Notes:

Disneyland Paris Travel Journal

Notes:

Disneyland Paris Travel Journal

Notes:

Disneyland Paris Travel Journal

Notes:

Disneyland Paris Travel Journal

Notes:

Disneyland Paris Travel Journal

Notes:

Disneyland Paris Travel Journal

Notes:

Disneyland Paris Travel Journal

Notes:

Disneyland Paris Travel Journal

Notes: